PATRICK O'BRIEN

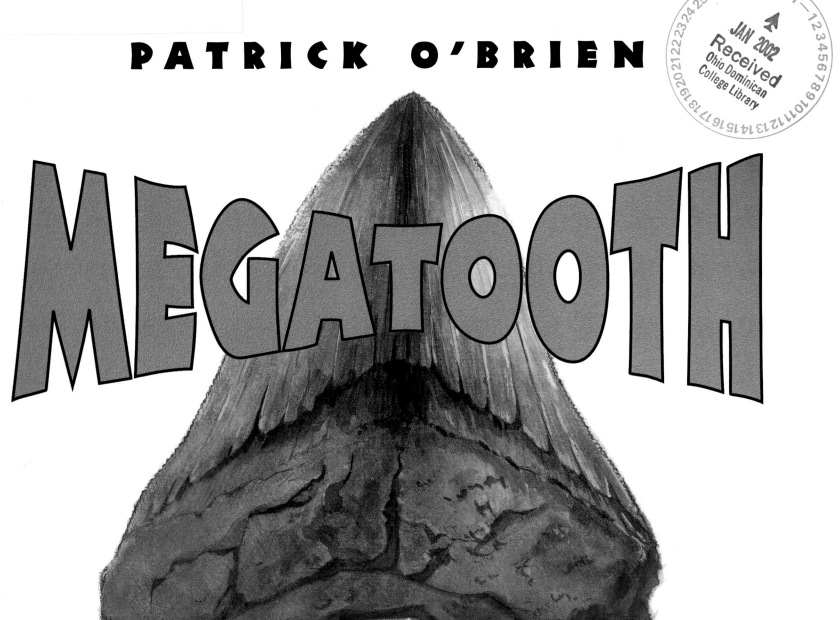

MEGATOOTH

HENRY HOLT AND COMPANY · NEW YORK

It was ten million years ago. Mysterious beasts swam the oceans. Strange creatures walked the earth.

It was a time of warm seas and steaming jungles.
It was an age of giants.

There were giant birds . . .

DROMORNIS
10 feet tall

. . . and giant horned turtles.

MEIOLANIA
8 feet long

There were huge beasts with strange heads . . .

MEGACEROPS
about 10 feet long

. . . and there were catlike hunters with giant saber teeth.

SMILODON
4 to 5 feet long

But in this age of giants, one giant ruled the seas . . .

MEGALODON!

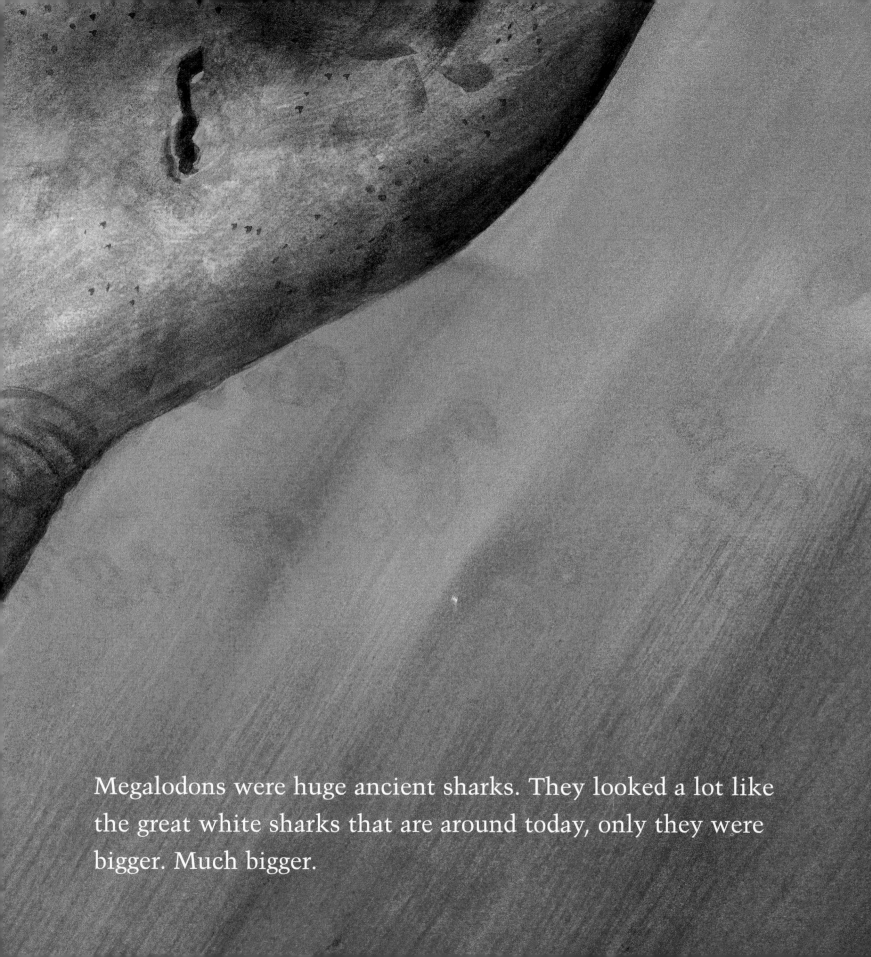

Megalodons were huge ancient sharks. They looked a lot like the great white sharks that are around today, only they were bigger. Much bigger.

GREAT WHITE SHARK
18 feet long

MEGALODON
50 feet long

Compared with the megalodon, the great white is a shrimp.

HUMAN
6 feet long

The megalodon was even bigger than Tyrannosaurus rex.

TYRANNOSAURUS REX
45 feet long, 5 to 7 tons

MEGALODON
50 feet long, 40 to 70 tons

Big, giant sharks had big, giant teeth.

Actual size

The name *megalodon* means "giant tooth."

And those big, giant teeth were in a huge set of jaws.

How do we know how big megalodons were? Well, it's partly just a guess. The only fossils ever found of these extinct sharks are a few vertebrae and some teeth. Lots and lots of teeth.

This is a view of the inside of a shark's mouth. Sharks' teeth begin to grow on the inside of the jaw. As they grow, they move toward the front of the jaw and are eventually shed.

Sharks produce many teeth throughout their lives, and they are constantly shedding the older ones. These teeth drop to the seafloor, and some of them become fossilized.

A fossil megalodon tooth looks much like a modern
great white shark tooth, only about three times bigger.
So we think that megalodons probably looked something
like great whites, but were about three times bigger.

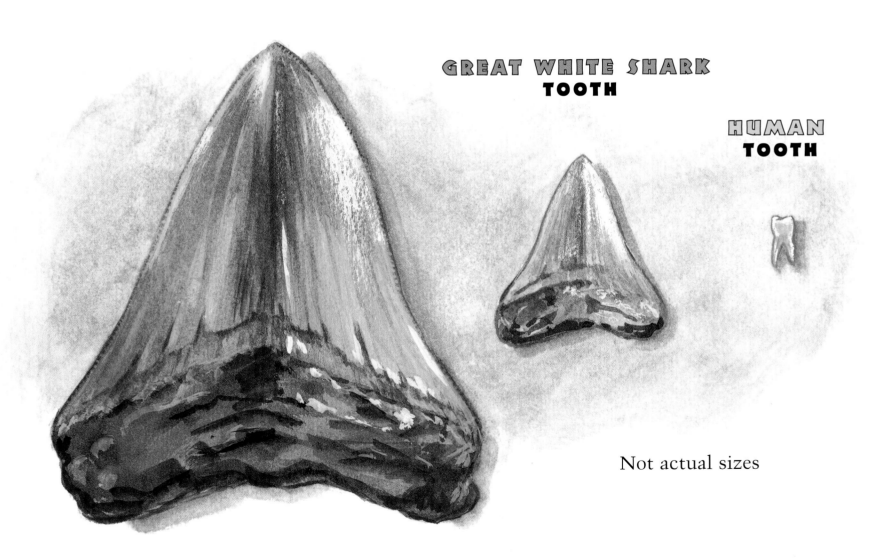

MEGALODON
TOOTH

GREAT WHITE SHARK
TOOTH

HUMAN
TOOTH

Not actual sizes

And what did a shark as big as the megalodon eat? Whales! Whales started to evolve from land mammals about 55 million years ago. Over millions of years, whales became bigger and bigger. Some scientists think that this was the reason the megalodons evolved to be bigger and bigger. They needed to be gigantic to feed on their gigantic prey.

Other giants have roamed the seas, but none were
as terrifying as the megalodon.

ARCHELON, a giant sea turtle

12 feet long
70 million years ago

ELASMOSAURUS, an aquatic reptile that
lived at the end of the dinosaur age

46 feet long
70 million years ago

SHONIOSAURUS, a swimming reptile
with a very dolphinlike body

49 feet long
220 million years ago

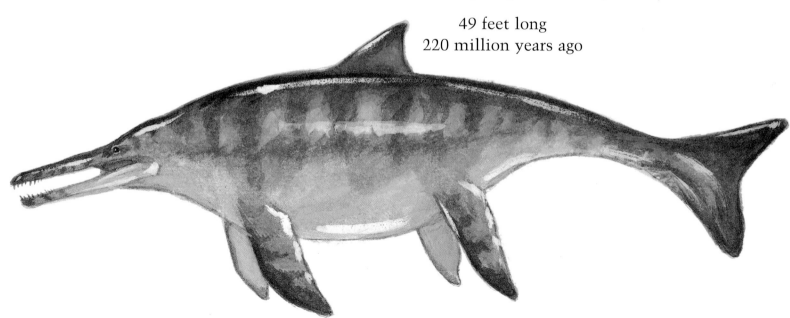

BASILOSAURUS, a primitive whale

49 feet long
40 million years ago

STELLER'S SEA COWS became extinct
only recently; these animals were killed off
by hunters in the 1700s.

up to 28 feet long

Scientists think that the megalodons died off about 2 million years ago. The earth's climate began to get cooler at this time, and so did the oceans. Perhaps the giant sharks just couldn't adjust to the colder waters.

Some people think that maybe the megalodons never died off after all. Perhaps they are still out there, and we just haven't noticed them—yet.

TIME LINE

This chart shows when different kinds of ancient animals lived. At the end of the Mesozoic era, all of the dinosaurs had died off. The land was left to the mammals to take over.

PALEOZOIC ERA **MESOZOIC ERA**

↑ 245 million years ago

↑ 65 million years ago

Some people call the Mesozoic era "The Age of Reptiles" and the Cenozoic era "The Age of Mammals." But sharks of one kind or another swam the seas during both eras. Maybe both eras should be called "The Age of Sharks."

CENOZOIC ERA

2 million years ago   present

THE TEETH

Really big teeth—that's about the only thing we know for sure about megalodons. But scientists can figure out how old these teeth are, and that shows them how long ago the megalodons lived. The oldest teeth found are about 24 million years old, and the newest teeth are about 2 million years old. So the megalodons lived between 24 and 2 million years ago. The dinosaurs were long gone by that time, but modern humans had not yet evolved.

Fossil hunters find these giant fossilized teeth all over the world. One of the best places to find them is the eastern United States. Sometimes a huge tooth is found sticking out of the soft rock of a seaside cliff. They may even be lying on the beach after a storm. The teeth are usually gray but are also found in shades of brown and red. They were probably white in the living sharks, but during the millions of years they were buried, they picked up color from the surrounding sand or rock.

Sometimes, in the same area as the teeth, whale bones are found that are scarred with giant tooth marks. That's one reason we think that megalodons ate whales. They probably also ate any large swimming beast that was unlucky enough to be nearby. A nice plump seal or a tasty giant squid would have made a good snack for a hungry megalodon.

Henry Holt and Company, LLC, *Publishers since 1866*
115 West 18th Street, New York, New York 10011

Henry Holt is a registered trademark of Henry Holt and Company, LLC
Copyright © 2001 by Patrick O'Brien. All rights reserved.
Published in Canada by Fitzhenry & Whiteside Ltd.,
195 Allstate Parkway, Markham, Ontario L3R 4T8.
Library of Congress Cataloging-in-Publication Data
O'Brien, Patrick. Megatooth / Patrick O'Brien.
1. Carcharocles megalodon—Juvenile literature.
[1. Carcharocles megalodon. 2. Sharks.] I. Title.
QE852.L35O37 2001 567'.3—dc21 00-28135

ISBN 0-8050-6214-9 / First Edition—2001 / Designed by Donna Mark
Printed in the United States of America on acid-free paper. ∞
10 9 8 7 6 5 4 3 2 1

The artist used watercolor and gouache on Italian watercolor
paper to create the illustrations for this book.